THE TRUMP REPORT

"Writings on the Wall"

Andrew Smith
(with Andrew Smith)

Copyright © 2017 Andrew Smith
All rights reserved.
Prime Prods Press, New York, New York
www.primeprodspress.com
www.andrewasmith.com
ISBN-13:
9780692856505
ISBN-10:
0692856501

Dedication

To Aaron Cohen

Friend, colleague, mentor.
He came up with the "with Andrew Smith" bit, so I had to do *something*.

CONTENTS

Preface vii

President Donald J. Trump: The First Hundred Days... 1
Selection of Questions and Answers from
    Sean Spicer's Press Briefings. 9
Trump Era Conspiracy Theories and Fake News 13
The Miniwall 17
Life Dilemmas for 2017 23
Merry Donald Christmas 2016 31
List of Other Trump Inspired Election-
    Related Recounts 33
Tiffany Tells it All. 37
New Secret Service Protocols for Protecting
    President Trump 43

Body Man 47
Discarded Chris Christie Campaign Slogans 53
Complete List of Proposed Trump
    Campaign Bumper Stickers 57
Questionable Questions for the
    Republican Debates 63
The Swoosh 67
2016 Presidential Campaign Nursery Rhymes 71
"My Dictionary" By Donald Trump 75
If Political Campaign Sloganeers Wrote Headlines
    for "Erectile Dysfunction" Medication Ads 81
"October Surprises" We Kinda Saw Coming 85
Scamilton: The Musical 89
New Trump Products 91
Consumer Products Militarized as Weapons By
    President Trump 97

PREFACE

Yes, *The Trump Report* which you now hold in your hot, little, short-fingered hands contains some previously published material. But there is actually some new stuff in there as well. I wanted to put it all together and get it out there before the subject in question left the scene. I figure we're talking a shelf life, here, of about equal to a fruit fly's retirement plan. But it's also why I kept the price down. The Sunday New York Times costs six bucks, for cryin' out loud. The only good thing about a book is that you can't wrap fish in it. You either have to keep it, or throw it away, or donate it to the Pequot Library and take a ridiculously high deduction. I suggest the latter. Then we'll be even. Sort of. Just don't give me any of that "I'll never get the time back" nonsense because I *know* how you spend most of your spare time.

Thank you for purchasing *The Trump Report*, and thank you for reading however much of it you could stomach before throwing it across the room in disgust. I hope it wasn't a *complete* waste of time and that you got a few laughs out of it regardless of which side of your head you part your hair on. (Donald parts his on the far left. Don't tell anyone.)

Andrew Smith
New York, March 2017

PRESIDENT DONALD J. TRUMP: THE FIRST HUNDRED DAYS

- First Lady now referred to as "First Piece of Ass."

- Disney forced to either retire Donald Duck or start calling it "The Donald Duck."

- Oval Office made square because it reminds the president too much of Chris Christie.

- Washington, D.T. instead of DC.

- "Hump Day" becomes "Trump Day."

- Strategic Air Command now "Fantastic Air Command."

- NFL forced to have a Super Bowl *every* Sunday.

- Department of Health and Human Services renamed "Department of Losers."

- Supreme Court now just the "Above-Average Court."

- All maps required to designate upstate New York as the "Extra-Long and Slender Finger Lakes Region."

- House Ways and Means Committee becomes the "House No-Way and Very Nasty Committee."

- The White House now "Trump House."

- All door knockers in Washington augmented with implants.

- Grand Tetons now the "Huge Tetons."

- Camp David now Camp Donald.

- Mar-a-Lago decorator appointed Secretary of the Interior.

The Trump Report

- Environmental Protection Agency is merged with Health and Human Services and becomes the "Department of Purell."

- Vice president renamed "loser low-energy president."

- POTUS now "POTRUMP."

- Skin cancer no longer called Melanoma out of respect for First Lady.

- Germs replace ISIS as the number one enemy.

- Megyn Kelly put on a no-fly list.

- Golf replaces baseball as the national pastime.

- "USS" designation for warships replaced with "Trump": From now on it's the "*Trump* Intrepid", the "*Trump* George Washington", etc..

- Field commanders ordered to say, "You're fired," instead of just "Fire!"

- Supreme Court justices are chosen via a special edition of *Celebrity Apprentice*.

- The Rose Garden is renamed "Trump Garden Place."

- Washington Monument becomes the "Trump Finger Tower."

- A "Jeb" is the new name for a drone.

- All official planes except "Air Force One" are called "Air Force Losers."

- Air Force One upgraded to "Air Force Definitely a Ten."

- Marine One helicopter grounded because of excessive windage and presidential hair damage.

- Secretary of Hair becomes a cabinet position. But the President refuses to call him, "Hair Secretary", because it sounds too Nazi

- UST not USA.

- President declares a National Day of Hair.

- Civil rights advocates sing, "We Shall Over Comb."

- Thanksgiving pardon of national turkey is replaced by apology to Carly Fiorina.

- DEFCON 5 declared if Rosie O'Donnell enters the Beltway.

- Closes down Federal Reserve; opens Trump Federal Casino.

- Seal Team 6 works security for all press conferences.

- "State of the Union" replaced with State of the Ego.

- Neutralizes Putin by sending Christie to stand behind him whenever he appears in public.

- Rejects gun control in favor of stricter hair control.

- First president to wear a baseball cap for his official portrait.

- Replaces White House fence with a wall. Mexico gladly foots the bill.

- Signs his first bill and is amazed it didn't cost him anything.

- Begins plans for Trump Presidential Library to house unsold copies of *The Art of the Deal*.

- Invades Chris Matthews.

- Finally realizes "The Situation Room" has nothing to do with *Jersey Shore*.

- Finally adjusts to living in a smaller house.

- Says to the navy guy carrying "the football," "You're fired!" North Korea is immediately bombed.

- United States files for bankruptcy—but not the president, personally.

- Yells, "Get him out!" at a protester in San Francisco. Two thousand people are immediately identified as homosexual.

- Tries to get his portrait on the twenty-dollar bill, but the engraver claims hair already looks engraved.

- Shocked when he finds out the Lincoln Bedroom is not named after a car.

- Every time he hears "The Star-Spangled Banner," he can't help thinking about Marla Maples in hot pants.

- Cancels the Easter Egg Roll because he wants to prove he's pro-life

- Gets face measured for Mount Rushmore.

- Changes name of White House to the "White-a-Lago."

- Orders golf carts to Afghanistan instead of Humvees.

- Celebrates Chinese New Year with a parade on Pennsylvania Avenue featuring a papier-mâché Rosie O'Donnell dragon and firecrackers.

- Redecorates the Lincoln Memorial with chandeliers.

- Asks Congress to approve a Trump golf course on The Washington Mall.

- New motto on currency: "In Trump We Trust."

- Nominates Stevie Wonder to administer his blind trust.

- "Hail to the Donald" replaces "Hail to the Chief."

- Log cabins are for losers. Official Trump birthplace designated a "Log Tower."

- Replaces red baseball cap with a red crown.

- Builds wall on Canadian border to stop Americans from leaving.

- Pardons Hillary Clinton.

- Creates cabinet-level position for personal barber but refuses to call barber "Hair Secretary" because it sounds too Nazi.

- Calls out Alec Baldwin for claiming to have done Trump more times than Melania.

- Confuses "Million Woman March" with open casting call for Miss Universe Contest.

SELECTION OF QUESTIONS AND ANSWERS FROM SEAN SPICER'S PRESS BRIEFINGS.

1) <u>Question</u>: Will President Trump ever go bald?
   <u>Answer</u>: Not as long as his intravenous Propecia drip remains attached.

2) <u>Question</u>: What's the matter with Kellyanne Conway's face?
   <u>Answer</u>: Instead of "Botox", Kellyanne had "Bowflex" injections. It didn't help her wrinkles, but she can press 250 lbs with her lips.

3) Question: What would happen if Mitch McConnell ever had sex with Elizabeth Warren?
Answer: The result would be a baby that looked like a turtle with a feather.

4) Question: Will President Trump ever run for a second term?
Answer: No. Second term abortions are currently against the law.

5) Question: Will Tom Brady and Giselle Bundchen stay married?
Answer: No. Tom Brady's "Deflategate" problems aren't just about his game balls.

6) Question: Is President Trump faithful to Melania?
Answer: Of course not. Look at what he's doing to the country.

7) Question: Will Michelle Obama ever run for president?
Answer: Yes. And her campaign slogan will be "Hype you can believe in."

8) Question: Will NASA ever explore space again?
Answer: Yes. President Trump just signed an executive order to build a colony on the red planet called "Mars-a-Lago."

9) Question: Why is president Trump against alternative energy sources?
Answer: President Trump and his barber have a pathological fear of leaf blowers and wind farms.

10) Question: Does Kellyanne Conway ever have orgasms?
Answer: Yes, and when she does, she cries out, "Oh, Sweet Trumpy! Yes!"

11) Question: Why did President Obama have such a poor relationship with the Russian Premier?
Answer: Obama mistakenly thought "Putin" was Russian for "Poontang".

12) Question: Will President Trump be successful in his promise to "drain the swamp" in Washington?
Answer: Yes. He plans to build a giant tampon (named after Megyn Kelly) and stick it in "Foggy Bottom".

13) Question: What will Hillary Clinton's next job be?
Answer: Leg model for Steinway.

14) Question: Will Steve Bannon ever be president?
Answer: Yes. Bannon will be president for as long as Donald Trump stays in the White House.

15) <u>Question</u>: Will President Trump ever convert to Judaism?
<u>Answer</u>: He may have to if he ever wants to marry Ivanka.

16) <u>Question</u>: Will Caitlyn Jenner ever complete her transition?
<u>Answer</u>: Yes. According to the TSA, Caitlyn is embarrassed that she gets an erection every time she gets "patted down" at the airport.

17) <u>Question</u>: Will Madonna ever win another Grammy?
<u>Answer</u>: Madonna will only win another Grammy after she becomes one.

18) <u>Question</u>: What Award did La-La Land finally win?
<u>Answer</u>: La-La Land won best film at the Speech Impediment Film Awards hosted by Lady Ga-ga-ga.

19) <u>Question</u>: What will Beyoncé's twins be named?
<u>Answer</u>: They will be named after the same fertility clinic that produced George Clooney's twins.

TRUMP ERA CONSPIRACY THEORIES AND FAKE NEWS

1) MELANIA TRUMP IS A CYBORG

2) CONNIE CHUNG AND GRETA VAN SUSTEREN ARE THE SAME PERSON

3) PRESIDENT TRUMP MODELS HIS HAIR THAT WAY BECAUSE HE THINKS IT MAKES HIM LOOK LIKE A BALD EAGLE.

4) PRESIDENT TRUMP STOLE HIS SIGNATURE RED TIE FASHION STATEMENT FROM PEE WEE HERMAN

5) THERE IS A DOCTOR AT THE HOSPITAL FOR SPECIAL SURGERY WHOSE EXPERTISE IS UN-DOING TRANSGENDER OPERATIONS. HIS SPECIALTY IS REPLACING THE ANCHOVY.

6) GLOBAL WARMING CAUSES WOMEN WHO ARE NOT PREGNANT TO SPONTANEOUSLY LACTATE.

7) SENATOR JOHN MC CAIN'S BAD ARM IS THE RESULT OF MASTURBATING TOO MUCH WHILE HE WAS A PRISONER IN NORTH VIETNAM.

8) THE ONLY REASON PRESIDENT TRUMP SUPPORTS WOMEN IN COMBAT IS SO THAT HE CAN PIN MEDALS ON THEIR CHESTS.

9) THE TRUMP ORGANIZATION WANTS TO HOLD A "CONGRESSIONAL MISS UNIVERSE CONTEST" IN WASHINGTON SO THAT THE PRESIDENT CAN SEE SENATOR GILLIBRAND IN A BIKINI.

10) FORMER DIRECTOR OF NATIONAL INTELLIGENCE, JAMES CLAPPER'S, REAL NAME IS "JAMES SYPHILIS", BUT HE HAD IT CHANGED TO AVOID BLACKMAIL THREATS.

11) TRUMP PLANS TO CONSTRUCT THE WALL ON THE MEXICAN BORDER USING THE ACTUAL BODIES OF MEXICANS AND OTHER IMMIGRANTS.

12) RANSOM NOTES FROM A HOSTAGE SITUATION INVOLVING MELANIA TRUMP WERE ACTUALLY WRITTEN BY MELANIA HERSELF EVEN THOUGH SHE'D ALREADY SIGNED A PRE-NUP.

13) THE SUCCESS OF CASEY AFFLECT AS A MOVIE STAR HAS BEEN ATTRIBUTED TO RUSSIAN HACKERS

14) DIET COKE ACTUALLY CONTAINS 1480 CALORIES MAKING IT THE MOST FATTENING LIQUID ON THE PLANET.

15) MC DONALD'S INTRODUCES THE "MC TRUMPIN" WHICH CONSISTS OF A SEAME SEED BUN BUT NO ALL BEEF PATTY ANYWHERE TO BE SEEN.

16) TRUMPCARE WILL PROVIDE "FUNERAL IN A CAB" AS A DEATH BENEFIT.

17) TIFFANY TRUMP HAD TO BE DISUADED FROM CHANGING HER NAME TO "MARY A

LAGO" SO HER FATHER WOULD PAY MORE ATTENTION TO HER ON THE WEEKENDS.

18) THE E.P.A. NOW STANDS FOR THE "ENVIRONMENTAL PISSING AGENCY" OR THE "E. PEE. A.". COAL MINERS AND OTHER INDUSTRIALISTS ARE NOW ENCOURAGED TO URINATE INTO THE RIVERS AND STREAMS OF AMERICA.

THE MINIWALL

EXT./INT. CROWD SCENES - DAY
MONTAGE: PEOPLE ON A CROWDED BUS. A CROWDED SUBWAY. A CHECKOUT COUNTER AT A SUPERMARKET PILED HIGH WITH GROCERIES. A CROWDED WAITING ROOM. A PACKED STADIUM AND THEATER. A JAMMED BUS. A PACKED CAR. A WIDE-BODY JET WITH EVERY SEAT TAKEN.

ANNOUNCER (*V.O.*)
Tired of being pushed, jostled, and having your space invaded by strangers or even friends and neighbors? Well, now there's something that can save you from all that.

GRAPHIC: ***PRODUCT SHOT:*** *"THE MINIWALL" (A SMALL, PORTABLE DIVIDER, EIGHTEEN INCHES BY SIX INCHES, THAT LOOKS LIKE A LITTLE BRICK WALL ON A STAND).*

ANNOUNCER (*V.O.*)
Introducing The Miniwall: A portable, reusable device that easily and effortlessly separates *you* from *them*.

INT. GROCERY STORE - DAY
ANNOUNCER (*V.O.*)
Use it at the grocery store...
A WOMAN PUTS THE MINIWALL DOWN BETWEEN HER GROCERIES AND THE LADY'S IN FRONT OF HER.

INT. BUS - DAY
ANNOUNCER (*V.O.*)
......Or on a bus...
A WOMAN PUTS THE MINIWALL DOWN BETWEEN HER AND AN ENCROACHING PASSENGER.

INT. BEDROOM - NIGHT
ANNOUNCER (*V.O.*)
....Or even in bed after a nasty fight...
A COUPLE GOES TO BED ANGRY. THE WIFE PUTS THE MINIWALL ON THE MATTRESS BETWEEN THEM.

ANNOUNCER (*V.O.*)
....Anywhere you want to avoid the unpleasantness of foreign co-mingling, interference, or alien infestation.

INT. THEATER - NIGHT
ANNOUNCER (*V.O.*)
Use The Miniwall at theaters....
A THEATER-GOER PUTS THE MINIWALL ON HER ARMREST.

INT, REST ROOM - DAY
ANNOUNCER (*V.O.*)
....public restrooms....
A MAN PUTS HIS MINIWALL UP ON HIS URINAL...

INT. DOCTOR'S OFFICE - WAITING ROOM - DAY
ANNOUNCER (*V.O.*)
....Or in a doctor's waiting room....
IN A CROWDED WAITING ROOM, A WOMAN PUTS UP *TWO* MINIWALLS ON EITHER SIDE OF HER.

INT. VARIOUS LOCATIONS - DAY
ANNOUNCER (*V.O.*)
.... on airplanes, in cars, or at stadiums...
SCENES OF PEOPLE TAKING THEIR SEATS IN CROWDED SITUATIONS AND PUTTING UP THEIR MINIWALLS.

ANNOUNCER *(V.O.)*
....Anywhere you just want to be alone and not have to deal with undocumented strangers *or* Muslims. And, best of all, in most cases....

INT. GROCERY STORE - DAY
ANNOUNCER *(V.O.)*
......you can make your neighbor pay for it.

INT. GROCERY STORE - DAY
AT THE SAME GROCERY CHECKOUT, THE CLERK FINISHES RINGING UP A SHOPPER'S GROCERIES. THEN SHE SEES THE MINIWALL ON THE COUNTER. SHE MISTAKENLY ADDS THE PRICE OF THE MINIWALL TO THE ORDER. THE SHOPPER IS AGHAST. THE MINIWALL OWNER NEXT IN LINE SMILES SMUGLY.

GRAPHIC: PRODUCT SHOT: THE MINIWALL.
ANNOUNCER *(V.O.)*
The Miniwall. Easier to use than a bubble. More convenient than a Haz-Mat suit....

GRAPHIC: STILLS OF PEOPLE UNCOMFORTABLE IN A BUBBLE AND HAZ-MAT SUIT.
ANNOUNCER *(V.O.)*
......And less controversial than a travel ban.

GRAPHIC: STILL OF CROWDED AIRPORTS AND REFUGEES
ANNOUNCER (*V.O.*)
At Miniwall, we believe that "Good Miniwalls make good neighbors."

INT. GROCERY STORE - DAY
THE SATISFIED MINIWALL OWNER HAPPILY PUTS HER MINIWALL BACK INTO HER TOTE BAG.
ANNOUNCER *(V.O.)*
(IN DISCLAIMER VOICE)
Void where unconstitutional or prohibited by law.

LIFE DILEMMAS FOR 2017

1. Ordering a Fruitcake When Your Waiter Obviously Is One

INT. RESTAURANT - DAY
TWO WOMEN ARE SEATED AT A TABLE IN A RESTAURANT. THE WAITER APPROACHES WITH A PAD AND PENCIL READY. HE IS DRESSED AS A COMPLETE FRUITCAKE.

WAITER
(IN AN OUTRAGEOUSLY FRUITY VOICE).
What'll it be?
THE WOMEN ARE MOMENTARILY TAKEN ABACK BY THE WAITER'S FRUITY VOICE AND FRUITY APPEARANCE.

WOMAN
I'll have the…
(STOPPING HERSELF)
….the thing with, you know, those little glazed, funny-colored bits and pieces in it…

WAITER
The what?

WOMAN
You know. The thing you get at holidays and never eat, and it just sits there in a can and gets hard all year long.

WAITER
I don't know what you're talking about.

WOMAN
Look. It's a baked thing…sort of like a loaf of bread…but it's not.   It's…more…cakey than bread…with little pieces of…well…fruit…in it. And it tastes great, but no one ever eats one. Apparently. *You* know what I mean. I'll have one of those.

WAITER
You mean a fruitcake?"

WOMAN
Yes!

WAITER
(TAKING THE MENUS AND LEAVING)
Why didn't you just say so?

2. Consensual Sex

INT. LIVING ROOM - NIGHT
A YOUNG COUPLE IS KISSING.

BOY
I love you.

GIRL
I love you, too.

BOY
I love you so much that I want to make love to you.

GIRL
I want to make love to you, too.

BOY
Great! Let's do it.

GIRL
(PASSIONATELY)
Yes, yes, yes! Take me. Take me.
The boy sits up and takes out a briefcase. He opens it and retrieves a folder of papers. Then he closes the briefcase and uses it as a desk.

BOY
All right, then. Now, honey, if you'll just sign here and here and initial here, here, and here…
The girl also sits up and seriously looks at the documents

GIRL
(CAREFULLY)
OK…But what if I change my mind in the middle?

BOY
No problem.
(TURNING PAGES)
That's covered here where I initialed. And look. I stipulated I'm STD- free and also…over here…that I've been without any other partners for six months. Signed, sealed, and notarized.

GIRL
(WITH AFFECTION)
Honey, you did that for me?

BOY
Uh-huh
(GETTING PASSIONATE AGAIN)
So, whaddya think?

GIRL
(SUDDENLY BORED)
I'm not in the mood.

3. Politics

INT. INSANE ASYLUM CHECKOUT ROOM - DAY
A MAN IS WEARING A CHICKEN SUIT WITH A STRAIGHTJACKET ON TOP OF IT. A DOCTOR IS TALKING TO THE MAN'S WIFE. THERE IS A SIGN IDENTIFYING THE PLACE AS "ASYLUM FOR THE CLINICALLY INSANE."

WIFE
Doctor, are you sure he's OK? Are you sure he's not crazy anymore?

DOCTOR
Oh yes, Mrs. Fenster. We've checked Mr. Fenster out extensively. He's been interviewed by the best doctors in the country. He's perfectly normal.

WIFE
But…the chicken suit…

DOCTOR
Well, Ralph likes to entertain. We see no problem.

WIFE
And the straightjacket?

DOCTOR
To tell you the truth, it was cold in here, and that was the only thing we had available. We *are* an insane asylum, after all.

WIFE
But…but he still seems completely wacko to me.

DOCTOR
Your husband is a great guy and a lot of fun.

WIFE
But how did you decide he was ready to rejoin society and live in the world like a normal person?

DOCTOR
Well, he very clearly announced to us that he wanted to be President of the United States. That clinched it for everybody. No problem.   Perfectly normal.

WIFE
(DUBIOUS)
OK. If you say so. Come on, honey. Let's go home.

MAN
Folks, I just wanna make America….
(À LA JERRY LEWIS)
….FLAMEN! again. Oh, LAAAAAADY!

MERRY DONALD CHRISTMAS 2016

President-elect Donald Trump wished the world a Merry Christmas on Sunday—on Twitter, of course. Trump tweeted out a #MerryChristmas photo of him with his right hand raised in a fist and a Christmas tree in the background behind him.

—CNN

Ten Alternative Trump Christmas Tweets instead of #MerryChristmas
(*over a photograph of Trump with raised fist in front of a generic Christmas tree*)

- Fantastic Virgin Birth. Very impressive.
- My thumb smells like Ivanka. Merry Christmas.
- Just fist-fucked Melania. Better than a Yule log.
- All I want for Christmas is a bigger fist.
- The Three Wise Men. They all voted for me. Get used to it.
- The Three Kings are fakers. Frankincense is for losers. Never used it.
- The manger was definitely substandard. Wouldn't have happened if they'd come to me first.
- For the same price, they could have stayed at a Trump Manger.
- As anyone can see, I've got a lot of balls at Christmas. A *lot* of balls.
- I only fist bump with God. Jesus is low energy. Sad way to try to save mankind.

LIST OF OTHER TRUMP INSPIRED ELECTION-RELATED RECOUNTS

- The exact number of Trump family plastic surgery procedures paid for by Donald J. Trump.
- Mar-a-Lago chandelier review.
- Trump blondness level re-calibration.
- Number of foreign-born nationals Donald Trump has had sex with.
- Trump administration white supremacist head count.
- Correct dollar amount of Trump's net worth.
- Number of abortions paid for by Trump before becoming a "right to life" advocate.

- Complete list of people personally insulted and maligned by Trump during the campaign.
- Final number of eye jobs for Melania.
- Lip-enhancement procedures for Tiffany.
- Ongoing lawsuits versus Trump.
- The true number of pantsuits owned by Hillary.
- The number of times Bernie Sanders has seen a barber in his lifetime.
- A complete list of Westchester County neighbors Bill Clinton has had sex with.
- A calculation of Trump's Twitter followers who actually possess a heartbeat.
- The total number of reinventions for Monica Lewinsky.
- The true number of non-releases of Trump's tax returns.
- A re-count on the number of Chris Christie's chins.
- Runoff figures between the use of "fantastic" versus "huge."
- The certified number of uses of "loser" as an epithet.
- The number of postelection Hillary Clinton deep-woods sightings.
- The final "bimbo eruption" tally.
- The adjusted number of Jared Kushner's "Mazel Tovs" to his father-in-law on election night.
- The correct number of Bernie Sanders's elocution lessons.
- Revised chances of Hillary being named Secretary of State in the Trump administration.
- Final number of Anthony Weiner's selfies and tweets cited in his divorce papers.

- Exact number of Trump family implants (male and female).
- Final tabulation of Electoral College votes, number of people at inauguration, and sad losers who leak.
- Number of Obama's Presidential Medal of Freedom recipients you would actually cross the street to see.
- Revised number of mentions of 9/11 by Giuliani.
- Number of emojis used in Hillary Clinton's top-secret e-mails.
- Percentage of Native American blood in Elizabeth Warren.
- Final number of times Joe Scarborough has changed his mind.
- List of objects carrying the Trump logo besides the Trump checkbook.
- Corrected number of times Mika Brzezinski and Joe Scarborough have had hot "makeup" sex during the campaign versus after the election.
- Eric Trump's IQ adjusted for wealth.
- Final number of Trump blood relatives with top-secret clearance.
- Number of times President-Elect Trump said, "Please, not now," about his daily security briefings.
- Relative ranking of Trump-owned businesses versus number of countries in the United Nations.
- Number of Trump cabinet appointees who have never seen a swamp much less drained one.
- Final count of Trump University graduates in the Trump administration.

- Recalibration of Rudy Giuliani's dentist's ranking on a list of top cosmetic dentists in the United States.
- Adjusted number of Tiffany Trump's motivational Instagram messages.

TIFFANY TELLS IT ALL
Tiffany Trump's Totally Fantastic Diary
"Make America Blond Again"

- OK. So I really don't understand why Eric and Donny and Ivanka got to be transitioning and not me. I mean, *c'mon*, I'm a college graduate. Who knows more about transitioning than me? I'm, like, practically Caitlyn level. I was transitioning in my friend Drew's fashion show. So why can't *I* have Top-Secret clearance? What am I, chopped pâté? *I want launch codes!* Maybe *I'd* like to launch something besides a new perfume line. I didn't even get my own Secret Service until November—*after* the election. Ivanka got hers in September. Bitch. "Top Secret" for Ivanka is lip gloss that doesn't smear. Why not me? I've got better hair. And more followers on

Instagram. Not like Daddy, of course. But all mine are actual people that I kinda know. No robots. You can't even talk to a robot. Unless you're drunk or partying with some other RKOIs.

- OK. So now that I have Top Secret clearance (which is *so* cool) and my own Secret Service guy and, also, all the super-cool launch codes. It's, like, so much better now, being around what is referred to as the *First* Family—meaning Eric and Donny and her highness, Ivanka. I'm the *Second* Family; and poor Baron, he's *Third,* and that doesn't count. It is so cool. I feel like I could launch a new single or something without Auto-Tune.

- Everybody knows Eric is as dumb as a tree. Look what he does with his hair. The straight-back wet look. Hel-lo! Loser! Anyway, I was talking to this cool navy guy from the government? The one who carries the football thingy, y'know? And I kinda winked at him and said, "Hey, handsome. I got codes, too. Howdja like to launch something together, maybe over a few Cosmos at midnight on some Washington beach and watch the sun come up?" Then he tells me that Washington, DC doesn't *have* a beach. And I say, "What-ever." And he says the grotty briefcase he has to carry all the time is handcuffed to his wrist. And I say, "Kin-ky! But I'm not into that…yet. I just graduated college. U of P. Don't ask."

The Trump Report

Yesterday, "Triple M"…that's "Marla Maples Mommy" to you, who is my BFF…and I *do* mean "F," really and truly, as in "Fabulous" *and* "Forever" and maybe "Fabergé," too. She's not allowed in the White House until she becomes a UN ambassador or whatever. But *I* am. I have my own room. I'm part of the official "First Family" now, and I'm not talking "The Three Kids of the Apocalypse" that Daddy got with Ivana. I call her the "Canceled Czech." Any*hoo*, Triple M and I went shopping and bought some clothes. I have to redo my entire wardrobe now to go with all the white. As in the *White* House? Hel-lo? Know what I mean? I mean, the Obamas were OK, but they sorta clashed. Dontcha think?

- Daddy calls it the "White *Again* House" now. But I think he had someone write that for him.

- And the Secret Service does *not* know how to do my hair. That's why I call them the "SS." Get it? So does Daddy. I like to have it sorta curled at the ends, you know? And blonder than Ivanka's. Because, c'mon. Truly, I have better hair than her highness, that Jew bitch. I call her, "I*wanna*." She is such a JAP ever since she converted. And Jared is so bossy. Even though I like the name Jared because it sounds so RKOI. But sometimes I think they shoulda locked *him* up instead of his dad. Did you see how he just waited, very cool, like he was Michael Corleone, until Daddy got elected before he made his move? Now Mr. Crisco sleeps with the fishes. Jared was so mean to fatso Christie just because of the jail thing with his dad. I mean, c'mon. Bygones, people!

- Do you think my lips are too fat? People think I'm mainlining Botox or something, but I'm not...anymore. I would kill for some cheekbones. Maybe I could have them put in like Barbara Walters did. Or I could use that lip cream, Pillow Plump. You can buy it at Duane Reade. And it is so cool. My lips are like blimps now.

- Anyway, do you know how cool it is to have a room in the White House...I mean, the "White *Again* House"?

- Anyway, you would *not* believe what goes on in the crazy world I'm in now. I mean, those briefings! Sitting there with Daddy and a whole bunch of foreigners, it's like binge-watching CNN or something. But don't ask. I can't say a thing. Top Secret, dontcha know. Doesn't that sound like a game show? Top Secret? But it's *really* serious. I couldn't even share what I know with a Kardashian. The stuff is that totally secret. Wow! And I never even heard of some of the countries we're going to bomb.

- Omigod! What's the big deal about immigration? I mean immigration is the highest form of flattery, isn't it? I mean, c'mon, people!

- I *love* my Secret Service guy now. It's like having a date but not as grabby. And he's, like, very *government*, y'know? Not my type. But sweet. Like a guard dog that you don't touch 'cause it might set him off. (Just like Dad.) He's Second Amendment all the way. He showed me the little gun on his ankle. Cool. And soooooo cute. We're an "open carry" family now.

- Well, toodles. Gotta go teach Melania how to say the Pledge of Allegiance in public. Whenever she puts her hand over her heart, all she can feel is the implant.

NEW SECRET SERVICE PROTOCOLS FOR PROTECTING PRESIDENT TRUMP

- Homeland Security level "hand check" required on any pussy within grabbing distance of POTUS.
- No leaf blowers on White House grounds when POTUS is in residence and not wearing a hat.
- Rosie O'Donnell on permanent no-fly list.
- Rose Garden appearances allowed only when weather service reports winds at "calm" or below.

- Senator Kirsten Gillibrand to wear swimsuit for Oval Office access.
- Thanksgiving turkey to be pardoned but not ridiculed.
- Cancel all performances of Pink Floyd's "*The Wall.*".
- Nuclear codes briefcase (i.e."The "Football") to also contain extra Purell.
- Rotors removed from Marine One helicopter.
- White House dog chosen from Miss Universe losers.
- Airport scanner for all finger augmentation products entering the White House.
- Angela Merkel and Theresa May never allowed to stand within one hundred yards of Melania.
- Background checks required on all barbers.
- No convertibles in presidential motorcades—ever.
- In case of assassination attempt, only female Secret Service agents with a rating of seven or above allowed to throw themselves on the President.
- "Drain the Swamp" to include Megyn Kelly's menstrual cycle.
- White House fence replaced with wall as gift from Mexico.
- Washington Monument renamed "Trump Finger."
- Doors of presidential limo fitted with childproof locks to prevent unsupervised egress.
- President's tweeting thumbs designated "weapons of mass destruction" and fitted with infrared sensors for twenty-four-hour monitoring.
- White House "Situation Room" moved to Jersey Shore.

The Trump Report

- No-fly zone to include President's trousers.
- West Wing designated "Absolutely *Best* Wing".
- White House Wi-Fi shut down at 6:00 p.m.
- "Trump U" is considered an expletive and threat and now deemed a federal offense when shouted within earshot of the President.
- "Top-secret" clearance removed from First Lady to prevent unauthorized copying.
- Waterboarding reclassified as a Presidential water sport.
- Border Patrol now in charge of the White House fence.

BODY MAN

A body man accompanies the politician or candidate virtually everywhere, often arranging lodging, transportation, or meals and providing companionship, snacks, a cell phone, and any other necessary assistance.

—Wikipedia

Never thought I'd end up a body man, but here I am. It's a good job. Steady. Like, no one bothers you. That's *your* job. *You* do the botherin'. "Wait, lemme get that," I say about twenty times a day. It could be a thread, or worse—the guy mighta sat in somethin'. That's when I think, *I really shoulda gone to business school.* Maybe next year. Right now, I'm lookin' at all these telltale sweat beads gatherin' on his upper lip. But I'm cool about it. I don't make no overt move. I don't do that. What I do is go up to the guy real close—*too* close unless you're the body man, if you know what I mean. *Real* close, and I look him right in the eye and hand him a handkerchief—linen, hemmed, no bleach, just the way he likes 'em. Then he gets the idea and appreciates I did it so nobody could see it. That's my job. Early warning system. NORAD with a handkerchief. I got eyes that penetrate every situation. Then he takes the handkerchief, pats down his upper lip, and hands it back to me. I take it like it was mine. I don't care. We're like brothers. Same cooties. Mission accomplished. Seal Team 6 got nothing on me. I know what that's all about. Service to a higher cause and invisibility. Boom! I'm outta there, and nobody ever noticed me, even though I was in plain sight. That's my job.

The governor really needs *two* body men. It's a big job in more ways than one, and I know what you're thinkin'. It's not just the size of the guy; he's a big personality—like Donald Trump if Trump were a nice guy. Trump has a body man. He has to. I can spot the signs. He probably has one who does nothin' but hair, but you never see him. *Never*. The governor's hair is easy. Bim, boom—over and out. But Trump has other issues. C'mon, get serious. Like he's a germ freak in public life. A body man's worst nightmare. In cases like that, the *body man* needs a body man because the guy isn't too sure about *you*, either. For all I know, Trump's got *three* body men. One just to take care of the other two so the guy doesn't get all freaked out over germs on his *number one* body man. Hey, think about that. A body man's body man. What's *that* all about?

Anyway, the governor's a great guy. I'd like to think I'm his friend, but I know I'm not. *Food* is this guy's friend. I've seen the look on his face when he gets near a buffet. If it was between me and a rack of lamb, I'd lose. Big time. I know that. When you're a body man, you know your place in the scheme of things. The guy has food issues. That's pretty obvious. My job is to make sure those food issues don't spill over into a legislative session in Trenton—or worse, onto his tie. Or maybe the food thing is reflected in statements at a town meetin' that could prove embarrassin' to the guy and undermine his effectiveness as the elected leader of the Garden State. But what's good for the governor ain't always good for New Jersey. Sometimes I'm the only thing between him and a tiramisu during negotiations with the teachers' union. But it ain't gonna happen when I'm around. That's what I get paid for. No crumbs, no smear, no dollop, no nothin' on the guy's fat face when he's doin' state business. You will *never* see him wipe his mouth with the back of his hand when he's raisin' tolls or chewin' out some caller on a radio show. I've had people say to me, "When *does* he eat?" That's how good I am as a body man.

Even when the guy had his Lap-Band surgery, he was real cool about it. No big deal. Coulda been just a couple of traffic cones across his duodenum for all anybody knew.

Next thing you know, the job is done. Just like that. "Time for some traffic problems in the large intestines," the surgeon probably said. Everybody's a comedian.

But don't get me wrong. The governor's a big guy. I mean, a *big guy*. That's how I got the job. I used to be a crane operator at a container facility in Elizabeth. I was handpicked when they needed someone who could handle a guy like that after he became a candidate and not just a prosecutor putting people away. But don't start with the "beep, beep, beep" jokes every time the governor backs up. We've heard all that.

But the guy *could* use some lights back there. I feel like I'm workin' on a freakin' national monument over here. I'm handlin' undershorts as big as the Hoover Dam. There's enough leather in one of his belts to put shoes on a family of five. I wish my apartment was as big as the seat of his trousers. I'd be livin' in a floor-through. I always carry five shirts for the guy. He likes to sweat. I don't want to say "like a pig." That's disrespectful. Let's just say you could corner the bacon market with an option on this guy's belly. Anyway, the guy's collar size starts with a "two." OK? He has a neck that's measured in furlongs, not inches. Horses could run around it at Monmouth. Bam!

I say all this so you get an idea of what I'm up against as the governor's body man. I should wear a Smokey the Bear hat, only that would give me away. Sometimes it's more like bein' in the high-risk catering business than anything else. The man likes to eat. Lemme tell you somethin'. The most dangerous spot in America is standin' between him and lunch. Once I brought him a beautiful Black Forest ham and swiss with lettuce, tomato, and mustard on seven-grain bread (he only eats rye on the "trail" for the Jewish vote). The guy bit right through the wax paper like a horse. Didn't even look at the sandwich itself until it was half-eaten. Then he says to me, "Where's the pickle?" and I say, "In your stomach, Governor, all nicely wrapped the way it came." I've seen him eat the panties off a lamb chop like he was Roman Polanski or somethin'. That's when I turn away out of respect.

My main job is to make sure none of the food stays on the governor after he's finished. That would be curtains for me as a body man and for him as a serious presidential hopeful and governor of a swing state. Nobody knows this, but sometimes the guy's chin looks like a landfill. See? Nobody knows that because I take care of it for him. I have a special "Wet One" that's just for his chin and some carbon tetrachloride wipes for his tie and lapels. City Harvest should make a stop there.

Look, I'm the governor's body man, and even *I* don't know how he got that fat. He was that way long before me. They should call him Governor Crisco, if you ask me. Let's put it this way. He didn't get that way from just breathin'. It's called *food*, dummy. Craft services got nothin' on me. A disposal is anorexic compared to what goes down *this guy's* throat. He never met *nothin'* edible he didn't like, includin' a couple of things hitherto known as *inedible*, if you know what I mean. Don't press me on this, but if he was a dog, then you'd have to take him to the vet to get an operation to remove some of those things, *pronto.*

Sometimes I'm a little jealous of the body men who travel with just a comb and a lint roller. Me? I'm like the guy who had to do cleanup after the loaves and fishes. He's a walkin' one-man Puerto Rican Day Parade. Every time he kisses a baby, I think he's gonna *swallow* it. Now, there's a vote getter. Takin' a bite outta an infant. Jeez! Anyway, it's pretty steady work, so that's a good thing. And who knows? Maybe the guy goes all the way. The next thing you know, I'm doing body work in the White House. But them state dinners there could be a nightmare. Maybe I should go on a diet myself first.

DISCARDED CHRIS CHRISTIE CAMPAIGN SLOGANS

- Let Me Eat Cake
- The Only Thing We Have to Fear Is No Buffet
- I Like Food
- Frosting You Can Believe In
- Keep Dinner Reservations Alive
- Turning Swords into Forks
- Two Chickens on Every Plate
- Feel the Bulge
- Let's Get America Snacking
- The Longest Journey Starts with a Decent Meal
- Christie Kreme

- Power to the Lunch
- Give Cheese a Chance
- Remember the Crème Brûlée
- The Mallomar Stops Here
- Stay the Three-Course Meal
- Cheesy Fondue and Crab Cakes, Too
- Don't Change Forks in the Middle of a Meal
- Ma, Ma, Where's My Pie?
- Four More Helpings
- We Want Dessert
- Peace and Profiteroles
- It's the Lemon Meringue, Stupid
- Yes, We Can Stuff Ourselves
- Breakfast Again in America
- Read My Lips: No More Dieting
- Are You Better Off Than You Were Without Syrup?
- Dinner First
- Eat, Baby, Eat
- In Your Heart, You Know He's Got Cookies
- Keep Cool and Keep Eating
- Putting Dessert First
- We Want Seconds
- Give Me Liberty or Give Me Lunch
- He Ain't Heavy, It's Just My Back Fat
- Win with Snacks
- Keep Cinnabon Alive
- Move Forward at the Buffet
- Christie Delivers Takeout

- Power to the Pie
- Nobody Can Swallow Trump
- Don't Change Lanes in the Middle of a Bridge
- Bypass Trump, Vote for Christie
- I Am Not a Whore
- Fewer Indictments than Hillary
- Chris Christie, for Chrissakes
- Sweatin' for Christie
- Food You Can Believe In
- Make Chris Christie Fat Again

COMPLETE LIST OF PROPOSED TRUMP CAMPAIGN BUMPER STICKERS

- Vote for Trump
- Trump for Trump
- Melaniamania
- Why Vote When You Can Trump?
- Give Me Trump or Give Me Everything
- I Trump
- Me!

- Hair You Can Believe In
- Hair Today, Prosperity Tomorrow
- If the Comb-over Don't Fit, Fuhgeddaboudit
- Pout This!
- I Do, I Do, I Do
- The Trump Wall Is for the Kool-Aid Man, Too
- Trumpica the Beautiful
- Star-Spangled Trump
- A Comb-over on Every Head
- You're Trump till Trump Says I Love Trump
- Don't Be a Wimp, Vote for Trump
- Trumpamemnon
- Trumpettes for Trump
- Trump Hair *Do*
- Trump, the President
- United States of Trump
- Put Trump in the Trump House
- Trumping in America
- Give America a Good Trumping
- "Trump, Trump, Trump," the Boys Are Marching
- I Hump Trump
- No More Apprentice
- I Thunka Trump
- Triple or Nothing
- A Trump in Time Could Save This Loser Country
- Stump with Trump
- I'm Rich
- Millions You Can Believe In
- I'll Find Obama and Take *Him* Out

- Our Future Is Trump, Not Rosie
- I Like Trump
- Trump *I* Can Believe In
- With Liberty and Justice for Trump
- For a Good Time, Call Lindsey Graham
- The Hair's the Thing
- Go Trump Yourself
- Me Again!
- Did I Say Trump?
- Ivana, Ivanka, & Trumpy, Too
- Set Your Hair on Fire with Trump
- Dominate with Trump
- Give Me Trump, or Give Me Trump
- I Have Not Yet Begun to Trump
- Don't Give Up the Trump
- Cling to the Trump
- Did I Say I'm Rich?
- Put My Money Where Your Vote Is
- I'll Buy Your Vote
- I Want *You* to Roll Over
- Money, Money, Money
- Had Any Trump Lately?
- Have It Trump's Way
- You Deserve a Trump Today
- Trump Me Once and Trump Me Twice and, Fuck It, Trump Me Once Again
- Real Trump
- A Trump among Men
- The Real Thing's the Real Trump

- If You Haven't Anything Trump to Say, Don't Say Anything at All
- Trumpin' in the Mornin', Trumpin' in the Evenin', Trumpin' in the Summertime
- I've Got a Feeling I'm Trump
- 2016 Trumpolympics
- It's Only Trump
- Don't Trump till You See the Whites of Their Eyes
- Show Me the Trump
- Money Can't Buy You Happiness, but Trump Can
- Better than Viagra
- Purell in Every Pot
- Hair Apparently
- Only Trump Will Tell
- A Trump in Time Saves Nine
- The Only Trump We Have to Trump Is Trump Itself
- It's Trump Time
- You Lookin' at Trump?
- Trump or Nothin'
- Seal It with a Trump
- It's Not a Vote until I Say It's a Vote
- You're Voted
- Get Fired Up
- The First President to Move into a Smaller House
- I've Never Been More Serious in My Life
- Elect Me, and I'll Prove I'm Electable
- From the Boardroom to the War Room
- "Comb" over to Trump

- The Best Things in Life Are Trump
- Trump I Can
- The Audacity of Trump
- What, Me Trump?
- Vote Trump till It Hurts
- Vote for the One with the Fringe on Top
- Lies You Can Trust

QUESTIONABLE QUESTIONS FOR THE REPUBLICAN DEBATES

- Who's smarter—a rocket scientist or a brain surgeon?

- Which candidate do you think Donald Trump's hair would look better on?

- Has anyone ever heard kids playing in a swimming pool and calling out, "Marco…Rubio?"

- Which candidate's penis looks more like Florida? Bush's or Rubio's?

- If the debates were an episode of *The Bachelorette*, who do you think Carly Fiorina would give her final rose to?

- Since Jeb Bush claims he's Hispanic, do you think he ever slips into Spanish during sex with his wife—as in "*¡Ay Caramba! Tú tan caliente, mami. Ya voy!*"?

- Quick: "Governor or cab driver?" Huckabee, Jindal, Kasich, Walker, Gilmore, Bush, or Christie?

- If they all wore dark glasses, which candidate would look like a Secret Service man guarding the other candidates?

- Rick Perry recently started wearing glasses. Should Trump sport an eye patch?

- Which came first—a place called Hope or political ambition?

- Rick Perry once owned a hunting lodge called Niggerhead. Is that like Jeb Bush calling his family's retreat Kennedybunkport?

- Where are the Ted Cruz "birthers"? Or do we *like* Canada?

- Trump always wears a baseball cap when campaigning. Is wind is more dangerous than Muslims?

- Rand Paul just wears that curly thing that sits on top of his head. Which candidate is hiding more? Trump or Paul?

- Is it true that associates of Donald Trump often refer to him as Mr. T and then imitate him, saying, "I pity the war hero"?

- Has anyone figured out that President Pataki is too much of a mouthful?

- How long before Ben Carson says, "This isn't brain surgery?"

- Is Chris Christie's bypass surgery just another lane-closure gambit for some "traffic problems in the duodenum"?

- Is Lindsey a girl's name?

- What's the difference between Santorum and a sanatorium?

- If war broke out between the Republican candidates, which candidate would have the most guns?

- Did you know that Ego is the name of a power source company *and* a hair treatment product?

THE SWOOSH

I can't tell you what I do. And I don't have to. OK? Personally, I have no use for the Freedom of Information Act. In fact, I don't need it. For me, it's more like the Freedom of *No* Information. So let's get that straight right at the outset. That's right. No information. In my experience—and I have plenty, by the way—information is never free. It costs money. A lot of money. So don't make me spell it out for you just because you're an idiot. Pay attention and maybe you'll learn something. I happen to do something every day that has a tremendous impact on America, and how, at least for my money, we could all look great again. But I'm not going to play games with you. Frankly, I haven't got the time. Some people say I tell it like it is. But that's another lie. I simply tell it. Period. The "is" is something that takes care of itself. I let the chips, and clips, fall where they may.

I do something—but I'm not going to tell you what it is because, frankly, I don't have to. It's none of your business. It's nobody's business. I don't need to tell people what my job is and especially how much I get paid to do it. But I will tell you this: I make a lot of money. A *lot* of money. And I'm proud of it. And I'm worth it, simply and very honestly, because I know how to get the job done. I'm one of the few people anywhere who knows how to deliver the goods, who does what he says he's going to do. Make no mistake about it. End of story.

Some people call me a barber. But that's their problem, not mine. I can't help that *or* them. I don't have a problem. Do you have a problem? *Somebody* has a problem. I only know how to do one thing, but I do it better than anybody else in the world. My client happens to have a great head. Maybe even the greatest. What I do isn't rocket science, but it *is* magic. Make no mistake about it. And that's what I get paid for. When I go to work, things happen. I haven't got time for chitchat, friendly or otherwise. Mostly otherwise.

It's an everyday job. Every day. I don't even take Christmas off. Neither does he. When he works, I work. And when he doesn't work, I *still* work. But that's what it takes to get the job done, and I'm all about getting the job done and getting it done right. It's pretty simple, really. He's got the ideas; I've got the technique. That's why we're a team. Him, without me, doesn't work, and that goes for the other way around, too. Anyone who makes a crack about the end result or puts it down just because of their simple lack of intelligence doesn't know the facts. You don't become rich and famous by putting your head in the sand. You make money by putting your head in my hand, which is more like it.

Anyone who thinks this is easy is a loser and is seriously kidding themselves, because it's not a comb-over. It's a sweep, a swoosh. But it also happens to be an entirely different thing. I tell Phil Knight that every time I see him, and I see him very often. Mostly for business. I haven't got time to explain the difference or the technique if you don't already know it. And if you don't know, then I feel sorry for you. I really do. You'll have to trust me on this. I'll deal with you and your obvious lack of a simple understanding of the facts later. It is what it is. Maybe even *I* don't understand what it is that I do that just happens to be incredibly unique and very effective and truly revolutionary in many ways. But I don't question it. I reap the benefits. That's what America is about, or used to be. Let's be honest: everybody else's hair stinks. Rand Paul came to me and begged me to give him pointers. I was happy to do it, but I told him I don't make a habit of this. He said it was charity. I agreed with him. He asked, and I gave. Three years later, I call him for some contacts, and he's there for me.

Look. It's very simple. I'm the only one who knows what he's doing. The rest are fakers and idiots. You don't have to believe me, but you *do* have to pay attention to me because I'm right, and you know it. I don't need this. I've got plenty to do. I could be cutting very wealthy children's hair at Paul Molé on the Upper East Side and making seventy dollars a head. But I care about this country and also about the future, which is where we're all going to be whether you happen to agree with me or not. Every time I perform an engineering feat with nothing but a few strands of hair—a feat that would make even Steven Spielberg faint—I'm doing it for America. What could be better than that? If the front of his head looks like it's constantly out of focus, then I've done my job. If you can't tell where the swoosh starts or where it ends, I'm a happy man. I'm a builder. I make things.

That's what separates me from anybody named "Tony." The four stupidest words in the English language as far as I'm concerned—and truly, I *am* concerned, and I know what I'm talking about—are: "A little off the top." Trust me. No one ever became great doing anything "a little off the top" or a little off anywhere, for that matter. That's where I draw the line. It's where I make my "part" in the sand, so to speak. The swoosh wants to be onhis face without being in his eyes. No easy feat. Spray is not the answer. It's all about style. Pure and simple. Style and a little engineering magic known only to me and a crane operator from Canarsie.

And, no, I will not lend you my comb.

2016 PRESIDENTIAL CAMPAIGN NURSERY RHYMES

HILLARY BILLARY
Hillary Billary's docs.
Her servers don't have any locks.
Her e-mails are tossed,
Top secrets are lost.
Hillary Billary's docs.

HUMPTY TRUMPTY
Humpty Trumpty
Sat on his wall.
Humpty Trumpty,
Spics paid for it all.
All the big donors
And all the white men
Couldn't put GOP together again.

KASICH HAD A LITTLE RUN
Kasich had a little run
But couldn't beat Mark Rubio.
And everywhere he ran, he lost,
Except, I think, O-hi-ee-o.

LITTLE MISS PALIN
Little Miss Palin
Sat on her tail and
Couldn't get into the fray.
So she posed with a boar
Shot dead by the whore.
Now Sarah's back in it to stay.

BERN AND JOE WENT UP AGAINST HIL
Bern and Joe went up against Hill
To fetch the Dem nomination.
Hill got indicted, and Bern got excited,
And Biden came stumbling after.

LITTLE BOY CRUZ

Little Boy Cruz
Come stow your horn.
Trump's in the White House
You still look like porn.

HEY, DIDDLE DONALD

Hey, Diddle Donald,
You'll never be Ronald.
Your hair is combed over your bloat.
The electorate laughed
To see such a dork,
And the Dems ran away with the vote.

BAA, BAA, BLACK DOC

Baa, baa, black doc
Have you any will?
No sir, no sir
I's still Trump's shill.

LITTLE CHRIS CHRISTIE

Little Chris Christie
Stood behind Trump
Eating his heart out instead.
Don gave him the thumb;
He won't get a plum.
He'd rather have someone like Jeb.

"MY DICTIONARY" BY DONALD TRUMP

Ballot (n.). Huge chance for some fantastic signage—for example, "The Trump Ballot."

Bankrupt (n.). 1. Some people are bankrupt. *I'm* not bankrupt. Have I ever been bankrupt? People have *gone* bankrupt trying to make me go bankrupt. But I have never, personally, been bankrupt. 2. Financial term meaning *partner*.

Barber (n.). Magician. Highest paid member of my staff.

Basic (adj.). Everything I know. Basically, I have a pretty basic knowledge of a lot of basic things. Basically, it's that simple.

Birth (v.). No problem, as long as it takes place in America. Otherwise, who's the mother? Do you know who the mother is? *I* don't know who the mother is. Somebody's the mother. Obama and Cruz were anchor babies, but not for this country.

Bombastic (n.). Normal, everyday speech.

Border (n.). Property line; wall footing.

Congress (n.). Losers.

Election (n.). A means by which millions of people get to choose me.

Everyone (n.). Some guy I pay for research.

Fantastic (adj.). Looks good, smells bad.

Fox (n.). 1. Wily, doglike animal known for intelligence and guile. 2. A very good-looking woman. 3. Conservative news outlet known for its blond anchors.

Germs (n.). Worse than ISIS. The real threat.

Golf (n.). 1. Good excuse for carrying a club. ("Speak loudly and carry a thin stick.") 2. Justification for environmental devastation. 3. Tricky way of limiting land use to only a few people who have actually paid me money.

Great (adj.). 1. Term used to describe me. 2. Did I say I was great? 3. Oh yeah, right. *See* "Like America *used* to be."

Hair (n.). A man's best friend. Better than a fourth wife. Hair is definitely a "ten."

Huge (adj.). Anything bigger than my mouth—for example, losses incurred by others while doing business with me.

Immigrant (n.). Campaign issue. *See* "Leaf blower."

Iowa (n.). State in the Midwest that starts with an "I," so it must have something to do with me.

ISIS (n.). Huge supporters. Without them, nobody would listen to me.

Lightweight (n.). Half a man—a "Trimp."

Look (v.). Imperative verb meaning "Pay attention to what I'm about to say because I'm going to insult you."

Loser (n.). Anyone who's not me—an "un-Trump."

Lot (n.). Much more than you have right now. In fact, a *lot* more.

Melania (n.). Chronic mental disorder characterized by thinking one's wife is the greatest beauty in the world and way better than Heidi Klum or Megyn Kelly combined.

Money (n.). Better unit of measurement than inches.

Poll (n.). 1. The only number that counts. 2. The thing in my pants. 3. What I wouldn't touch Rosie O'Donnell with even if it was a *twenty*-foot one.

Pout (n., v.). 1. My bitchy resting face. Holding the mouth in such a way as to resemble the act of kissing the mirror I'm standing in front of. 2. A silent way of saying, "I'm fantastic, and everyone knows it." *See* "Facial anus."

President (n.). I accept, but "Trump" has to come first. After the election, it should be "Trump President," not the other way around.

Primary (n.). 1. The main thing. It must have something to do with me. 2. A local election to ratify me.

Rosie O'Donnell (n.). Monster; an animal.

Schlonged (v., past tense). Beaten down and made to lie flat; totally collapsed and unnaturally folded over; lifeless, limp; appearing foolish and fake; an object of ridicule and disdain. *See* "Does this hair make me look fatuous?"

Sex (n.). Marriage proposal.

Size (n.). Always measured in penises, not fingers.

Trouble (n.). What everyone else is in except Donald Trump.

Voters (n.). Suckers. They'll buy anything.

White House (n.). Let's face it. A so-so guest cottage in Washington. Not luxurious at all. I bet the roof leaks. When I'm president, maybe *that's* where the wall should go.

IF POLITICAL CAMPAIGN SLOGANEERS WROTE HEADLINES FOR "ERECTILE DYSFUNCTION" MEDICATION ADS

- Keep Erections Alive
- Ask Not What Your Erection Can Do for You; Ask What You Can Do for Your Erection
- We Have Nothing to Fear but Erectile Dysfunction Itself
- I Like Erections

- We Want Erections
- Make Erections Great Again
- Tippecanoe and Erections, Too
- Are Your Erections Better Off than They Were Four Years Ago?
- The Audacity of Erections
- Yes, We Can Keep an Erection
- A Thousand Points of Erections
- Time for an Erection
- Four More Erections
- Heal, Engorge, Revive
- It's the Erections, Stupid
- Right to Rise
- New Possibilities, Real Erections
- An Erectile Revolution Is Coming
- Reigniting the Erections of America
- From Hope to Higher Erections
- Defeat the Washington Erectile Dysfunction; Unleash the American Erection
- It's Morning Erections Again in America
- Don't Swap Erections in the Middle of a Stream
- Happy Erections Are Here Again
- All the Way with BJ
- Yes, We Can Get an Erection
- A New American Erection
- Hillary for Erections
- Rebuild the American Erection
- Restore the American Dream for Hardworking Erections

- An Erection You Can Believe In
- Erections You Can Trust
- Ready to Have an Erection on Day One
- Erections for Us
- Reform. Growth. Erection.
- America Needs an Erection
- Let's Get Erections Moving Again
- A New Erection for a New America
- America's Top Erection
- The Better Erection for a Better America
- An Erection Called Hope
- Time for an Erection
- Building an Erection to the Future
- Moving Erections Forward
- An Erection for the New Millennium
- Give 'em Erections, Harry
- Grant Us Another Erection
- An Erection in Every Pot
- Erection Days Are Here Again
- Life, Liberty, and Erections
- Win with Erections
- I'm Just Wild about Erections
- Peace and Erections
- We Can Do Erections
- In Your Erection, You Know He's Right
- The Erection's the One
- To Begin a New Erection
- Erections: Now More than Ever
- A Leader for an Erection

- Where's the Erection?
- Kinder, Gentler Erections
- Erections for a Change
- It's Erections to Change America
- Putting Erections First
- Compassionate Erections
- A Stronger Erection
- Let Erections Be Erections Again
- Yes, We Can Have Erections
- Erections First
- Reform, Prosperity, and Erections
- Believe in Erections
- Restore Erections Now
- Erections Aren't Working
- An Erection to Believe In
- Feel the Erection
- Erections for America
- I'm with Erections
- A New American Erection
- Courageous Erections
- Erections Can Fix It
- From Erections to Higher Ground
- The Better Man for a Better Erection

"OCTOBER SURPRISES" WE KINDA SAW COMING

- Ivanka Trump, a recent convert to Judaism, decides to out-Malia Malia and take a JAP year.
- General Petraeus invades another mistress.
- Hillary Clinton wears a skirt.
- Larry David mounts a third-party candidacy from Vermont
- Gwyneth Paltrow gets treated for Goop.
- Beyonce's extensions get their own record deal.
- Donald Trump announces his hair is pregnant and gives birth to a 7.7-pound toupee. Donald is identified as the father. Apparently, he finally did what people have been telling him to do for years.

- Schwarzenegger's love child marries a Kennedy.
- A Kardashian enters a "for-profit" college but leaves when she doesn't get paid.
- The "DTs" are reclassified as an election-year-only disorder.
- The NFL investigation into concussions is expanded to cover domestic partners.
- Somebody kills Bill O'Reilly.
- Chris Christie removes the traffic cones that were placed across his small intestines by a trusted aide.
- *Hamilton* tickets are no longer scalped. They're "hedge funded."
- Bill Clinton has another bypass. This time he says no to a Westchester MILF.
- Bill Cosby launches a one-man show that is immediately considered the first suicide bombing by an American.
- The academy announces that, next year, the Oscar statue will have cornrows.
- Charlie Sheen admits his version of "streaming" has nothing to do with television.
- Caitlyn Jenner gets hired as a ball girl for the US Open.
- Kim Jong-un finally fires his barber.
- China establishes takeout on the disputed islands in the South China Sea.
- Jeb Bush demands a recount.
- Vice President Joe Biden announces there's nothing wrong with presidential implants.

- Rick Perry finally remembers that third thing he would have eliminated.
- Justin Trudeau vows to build a wall around Barbra Streisand.
- The Electoral College disavows Trump University.
- David Cameron starts referring to the EU as the "Eeeeeyuuuuu!"
- Bo, the unarmed presidential dog, is shot by a white DC police officer.

SCAMILTON: THE MUSICAL

BLOOMBERG
How does a bastard, slumlord, son of a bitch, and a German, dropped in the middle of a campaign for president,
Ridiculed and spewing so much Muslim hate
Grow up to be the Republican presidential candidate?

TED CRUZ
The $10 billion son of the founding father
Got a lot farther by working a lot harder,
By bein' a lot smarter,
By bein' a self-starter who liked to hump
By fourteen, so they placed him in charge of everything called "Trump."

OBAMA
And every day while immigrants were being deported and carted
Away across the waves, he struggled and kept his guard up.
Inside, he was longing for something national to be part of;
The brother was ready to beg, steal, borrow, or barter.

BERNIE SANDERS
Then 2016 came and devastation reigned.
Our man saw his country's future drip, drippin' down the drain.
Put a comb to his temple, made his hair look insane,
And he wrote his first refrain: *Let Mexico feel the pain.*

BLOOMBERG
Well, word got around, they said, "This guy's insane, man."
Took up donations just to end his presidential claim and
Stop saying you'll send Muslims back from whence they came and
The world's gonna know your name! What's your name, man?

TRUMP
Donald J. Trump, I am.
My name's Donald J. Trump, I am.
And there's a million things I haven't done.
But just you wait, just you wait.

NEW TRUMP PRODUCTS

TRUMP LONG JOHNS: Condoms for men who are yuuuuuge.

TRUMP SUN BLOCK: Guaranteed to never let you look like an immigrant.

TRUMP TIRES: Nothing with the Trump name on it ever goes flat.

TRUMPIALIS: Just the thing for men who can't get it up and be huge.

TRUMP SHEARS: Scissors that cut both ways.

TRUMPHONE: If you vote for me, you can call me.

TRUMPIES: Fifty-hour energy for after you finish the five-hour one.

TRUMPMOBILE: Car that runs completely on hot air.

TRUMP COMB-OVER CLUB FOR MEN: If I can get away with it, then you can get away with it.

TRUMP GPS: The most fantastic product ever for losers who get lost. Never be a lost loser again.

TRUMP AIR: Not the airline. I sold that. Is there a law against selling? I'm talking Trump *Air*. Air that I have actually breathed. Now you can breathe the same stuff, too, and not be such a loser.

TRUMP VITAMINS: Forget vitamin A and vitamin C. This is vitamin T. Specially formulated to make you more like me.

TRUMP IMPLANTS: Let me take you from a miserable Megyn 3 to a fantastic Melania 10.

BOTRUMPTOX: Inject me into your face so you don't have a "loser resting face."

TRUMP BRASS KNUCKLES: Just the thing for a nice, peaceful demonstration at a rally.

TRUMP HAIR COLORING: Blondes have more fun and do better in the polls.

TRUMP FLAGS: Get one now and avoid the rush. When I'm president, it'll be UST: United States of Trump.

TRUMP MATTRESSES: Negotiate with style *and* comfort on a Trumpopedic mattress.

TRUMP WEDDING CHAPELS: If I had one of these available to me, then I'd have ten marriages, not just three.

TRUMP LIPSTICK: For a pout that won't quit.

TRUMP OPTICS: See everything *my* way.

TRUMP, THE COLOGNE: It's the sweet smell of excess. For the man who wants to smell like money…a *lot* of money.

TRUMP GOLD: Why should gold be the most valuable thing? Trump Gold is *bette*r than gold. Gold is a loser.

TRUMP SCREEN DOORS: The most incredible screen doors you ever saw. They keep mosquitoes, flies, gnats, and beetles out. And anyone else you want to keep out, too. Works like a wall. They're fantastic.

TRUMP AVOCADOS: Not Mexican in any way, shape, or form. American avocados the way avocados were meant to be. You can rest assured.

TRUMP SPEAKERS BUREAU: Book someone who isn't afraid to tell it like it is. Basically, book me, Donald J. Trump.

TRUMP LOW-ENERGY PILLS: I developed these pills myself after debating Jeb Bush. Basically, they're pages of my book *The Art of the Deal* ground up into little capsules that are a lot easier to take than actually reading it.

TRUMP CHICKEN: OK, it's not chicken because Donald Trump is not chicken. Got that? And it's not turkey, either, because Trump is not a turkey. In fact, I don't have to tell you, or anyone else, what Trump Chicken is or isn't. But, folks, it tastes like chicken. Case closed.

TRUMP WONDER BRAS: You want to be a ten? Who doesn't want to be a ten? Everybody wants to be a ten. I'm a ten. Wear my bra, and you'll be a ten. Even if you're a guy.

TRUMP DIVINITY SCHOOL: Why worship a loser like God who does a lot of very bad things. Make no mistake about it. *Very* bad things. At Trump Divinity School, you worship somebody who can actually do something for you. Me!

TRUMP BASEBALL CAPS: I wear a cap, and you can, too. My caps come in only one color: red. Inside is a special hair revitalizer that conditions your hair for as long as you wear the cap. When you take it off—*voilà!* Instant swoosh.

TRUMPURELL ANTISEPTIC GEL: I hate germs. Do you hate germs? Somebody hates germs. I hate germs almost as much as I hate Mexicans. Sometimes I don't even know the difference. My Trumpurell will kill anything on contact. Especially Cubans.

TRUMP SWEAT SUITS: I don't sweat. Do you sweat? Somebody sweats. Trump sweats are "no sweat" sweats. Fantastic. Just the way I like it.

TRUMP RUNNING SHOES: Talk about a swoosh! If you're going to run, then you need fantastic running shoes. Trump running shoes are especially made to stomp on protesters and get 'em outta here! Make running Trump again.

TRUMP WINE: I don't care what year it is. If it's Trump Wine, then it's a fantastic year. Trump Wine is the finest wine ever made. And if you don't believe it, then you're drunk...unlike me, who has never touched a drop. I don't drink. I just *drive* people to drink.

TRUMP CHOCOLATES: The finest chocolates anywhere in the world. Dark chocolate, light chocolate, milk chocolate. The chocolates love me. Did I say Ben Carson endorsed me.

CONSUMER PRODUCTS MILITARIZED AS WEAPONS BY PRESIDENT TRUMP

- "Presidential Strength" hairspray weaponized as "Nerve Gas in a Can"
- "Preparation H" re-engineered as Claymore anti personnel pucker bombs.
- Toll booth change guns adapted to shoot high-velocity quarters that kill. (cheaper than bullets.)
- Self-driving cars adapted by the military for battlefield use. One problem: They keep going AWOL

- Do-It-Yourself transgender kits weaponized to instantly change the gender of any enemy combatant engaged in hand to hand combat.
- Self-driving cars re-deployed by the military as non-suicidal bombers.
- Non-Lethal Nerve gas transformed by LBGT scientists into a weapon that causes enemy combatants to declare, "You've got <u>some</u> nerve!"
- Helmet-grade toupees. Soldiers can fight and flirt at the same time.
- M-16 semi-automatic cell phone. Fires lethal "tweet bombs" with soldier's trigger thumb.
- Calvin Klein cologne thrower. A flame thrower that shoots "Obsession". Once that shit hits you, nobody wants to fight.
- Self-waterboarding water bottle. Water bottles weaponized into waterboarding refreshers that force thirsty terrorists to self-confess.

www.ingramcontent.com/pod-product-compliance
Lightning Source LLC
Chambersburg PA
CBHW070205100426
42743CB00013B/3055